Crops In My Lifetime

By

John E. Lewis

For my wife Shirley with my heartfelt thanks for her unfailing support and encouragement during the writing of this book.

PUBLISHED BY:
JOHN E. LEWIS
Spindlewood
19 Orchard Grove
Croyde
North Devon
EX33 1NF

Front cover: author outside Kittiwell   1949
Back cover: author on Saunton Down 2008

First published 2009
Reprinted in 2009

The British Library Cataloguing in Publication Data. A catalogue record for this book is available from the British Library.

ISBN: 978-0-9562758-0-6

Collated by Andrew T. Byrom

PRINTED BY WESTPRINT,CLYST ST MARY, EXETER EX5 1SA
TEL: 01395 233 442

CONTENTS

Acknowledgements

I am greatly indebted to Andrew and Jane Byrom for their freely given constructive advice and valuable time; for photographs, and the numerous hours spent collating this book, all very much appreciated.

My grateful thanks to Cecil Parsons who has an immense source of information relating to Croyde which he has willingly shared with me.

Also thanks to Mike Harrison who was always willing to assist in anyway and provided the detailed map which can be found at the back of the book.

My gratitude to Tony Evans, for compiling the introduction to this book and along with his local knowledge and advice, has made many suggestions.

Lastly but certainly not least I thank my friends for photographs, relevant information, their support and interest in this project:
John and Gwen Adams, Tom Bartlett Collection EX34 9SE, Brian and Janet Butler, Mick and Jill Comber, Pam Eveleigh, Gerald Fisher, Bill Foster, Reg Fowler, Susan Gibbs, George and Janet Hakin, Denise Hodges, Terry and Mary Hutchinson, Steve Knight (R.L.Knight Collection), Geoff and Pam Lang, Tom and Joan Lang, Steve and Jackie Lippiatt, Paul Madgett, David and Marcia Maddocks, Verley Meek, Braunton Museum, Peter and Alison Symons, Terry Welsh, Eirene Williams, Henry Williamson Literary Estate.
If I have missed anyone I apologise.

Introduction

Countless books have been written about farming and the countryside, but many have been written by those who, like me, have been mere observers of the rural scene, not participants as John Lewis has. Combined with numerous evocative photographs that enhance the narrative, it is written with empathy and an expressiveness that reveals a deep understanding of the farming life. And it is farming that forms the core of this interesting and informative book of life in a small North Devon coastal village, during the Second World War, and the succeeding years that followed.

The author takes us on a long and varied journey through his life; we read of his family, his wife and children, his father and mother's daily life, of how during the war and in the austere post-war years it was a case of make do and mend with anything that came to hand. We hear of the people he worked with, each and every one a character in their own right.

Here is a life that has been full of purpose and dedication, not just the author's devotion to the land and his family, but his resolve to help those in peril on the sea by way of being a member of the Auxiliary Coastguard Service.

Readers of this book who, like me, can recall those days will do so with a deep sense of nostalgia, will recall schooldays, and certain associations, bringing to the fore half forgotten memories; of how as children we were granted the freedom to roam the fields, the woods and hedgerows at will, seeking out in season blackberries, mushrooms, and hazel-nuts.

This is a record of how farming practices have changed dramatically in the last fifty years, of how during a period of transition shire-horses, those great gentle giants beloved and respected of the folk who cared for them, worked alongside the tractor.

We read of the steam traction engine and thresher which extracted the golden grain in the days before the combine harvester relieved the work of a team of men that sometimes included women. We are made aware of the hard manual work, of the diverse nature of that work, and the skill required of the so-called farm labourer, or agricultural worker, a term that is both misleading and demeaning. The man who worked on a farm at a time when manpower was king, before the machine took over and farming became more industrialised, was actually a master craftsman capable of achieving any job that was required of him. He could layer a hedge, build a dry-stone wall, hang a five barred gate, milk cows, administer to a sick animal, build a corn-rick and crown it with a roof of rainproof thatch.

John demonstrates how, through hard work and diligence, he was able to achieve a long-held ambition of buying a few acres he could call his own, an ambition which he achieved; with his wife Shirley, and at times their children, he worked the land, knew the farming year in all its moods and seasons, the rain, the bitter cold of winter, the stifling heat of summer at harvest time.

Life in this rural corner of Devon, as in all walks of life, has changed, but has it all changed? The answer must be no, only in part. The little school attended by John all those years ago continues to thrive. The village farmhouses are still there, but now play a different role, having become comfortable private dwellings while others cater for visitors who appreciate and enjoy a still beautiful and largely unspoilt corner of Devon.

Before memories begin to fade John set out to record something of his life and the people he has grown up and worked with. He was perhaps unaware that he was also composing an important social history of Croyde and its environs, but this is what he has accomplished, and so I thank him, and feel privileged in being granted the opportunity to be among the first to read this book.

Tony Evans: June 2009

Looking down Hobbs Hill with William 'Gunner' Budd on the right outside the barn of Burrows Farm c1920

Chapter I   MY FAMILY

My mother, Alice Gertrude Saunders, was born in Gibraltar in 1907 during a tour of duty for her father's work. He was a Regimental Sergeant Major in the Army. His wife died when my mother was about ten years old and the family returned to York. When her father re-married, the family split up and my mother went into service with the Rowntree family. She was originally taken on as a parlour maid – a temporary position as she was only 4'11" and a taller girl was preferred for this job. She graduated to the position of cook and came to Croyde with the family on their annual holiday. This is how she met my father.

My father, Charles Lewis, was born in Hobbs Cottage opposite 'The Thatch' in Croyde in 1903, one of six children: Charles, William, Wilfred, Mabel, Hetty and Rose. He lived all his life in the parish of Georgeham and after leaving school at eleven, he worked on various farms in the area. When we lived at Putsborough he worked at Manor Farm for Frank Tucker, he had also been employed at Castle Street Farm, North Buckland, with his brother William; later he worked at Baggy Farm. He always kept a few sheep and cattle of his own in fields around Croyde and he reared pigs in the out-buildings at the Thatched Barn (now re-named 'The Thatch') opposite where he lived.

Hobbs Cottage with Wilfred Lewis (my uncle) 1936

1

After being invalided out of the army, he was employed at Saunton Sands Hotel on general maintenance duties, walking over Saunton Down from his home at Wee Cott to get there, when it was occupied by the Duke of York Royal Military School from Dover, a boarding school for boys who were sons of service men or from soldiering families, many of them orphans. After being evacuated from Dover into temporary accommodation, they were finally moved to Saunton Sands Hotel in early 1941.

Duke of York Boys at Saunton Sands Hotel 1943

Austin Yeates (one of the Duke of York Boys far left) on Saunton Sands next to an American jeep 1944/5

This was a school for army cadets and my eldest brother George was a pupil there, returning to Dover with them after the war.

When the school closed my father became self-employed, he would buy wild ponies in the autumn, some from Bampton Fair and others from Lundy Island. Usually accompanied by George Symons and Donald Chugg, they would round up the wild ponies on Lundy Island and drive them to the beach where they were held in pens prior to loading. A sling was attached to each pony and they would swim them to the awaiting boat.

L-R. Donald Chugg, George Symons, my father
and others on Lundy Island. 1953

Sheep and bullocks were also transported in this way and sold at Barnstaple Market. Some years later, a landing craft from the army camp at Instow was used. This went right onto the beach at Lundy, making the loading of ponies much easier and once back at Instow they were transferred to awaiting cattle lorries. During the winter, my father broke in the ponies and used them during the summer at a riding school he ran in the mornings and on the beach for childrens rides in the afternoons. He would sell all of the ponies at the beginning of the autumn and then buy more wild ponies, starting the cycle all over again. Later he had donkeys instead of ponies for childrens rides on the beach.

My father at his riding school Croyde Bay c1950

My father taking his donkeys out to the beach c1965

4

William (Angel) Parsons and my father c1930

During the winter months he would also buy the rights to acquire all the rabbits on a certain farm, which he would shoot or trap then sell for human consumption.

My father had a dog called Spider who was very good at catching rabbits on a moonlit night. He taught Spider to bring back rabbits to him undamaged by using a rabbit skin, filling it with holly leaves and then sewing it up.

By throwing this 'rabbit' and getting Spider to retrieve it he taught him to bring the live rabbits back without crushing them. Spider was a one-man dog and didn`t like being away from my father; sometimes my brothers and I would put him on a lead (usually an old tie) and take him over the downs to see if he would catch a rabbit for us, but as soon as we let him go he would run home looking for his master.

My Father was a water diviner and he also dug various wells in the area. On one occasion, when I was young, I can remember being with him at Sandy Lane, Croyde. My father was digging the well and Bill Carder was winding up the stones and rubble as they went. The digging got tough and my father decided to use some explosives to dislodge the rock. He put the explosives down the well with a long fuse, which he lit after putting sheets of galvanised iron on top to contain the explosion. We quickly jumped over the hedge into Lang's Field and took cover! The noise was tremendous but did the trick and my father finished digging the well and Bill Carder walled it up. Father sold five sites in the field, on which chalets were built. The well water was used until mains water arrived in the village and I understand the well is still there, capped. He also dug a well at the end of Cott Lane and when he got down to approximately twenty six feet digging through layers of earth, sand, gravel, and lastly pebbles, he came across two lengths of wood, they were laying east to west the same way as the spring was running. One was oak and the other was pine and both were about four to five feet in length. This well water was used by Mr and Mrs Boyde at the Croft, Cott Lane, until the mains water was connected.

St. Mary's Road outside May Cottage. June 1931
L-R Fred Dawes, Bill Miles, Fred Gammon, Bill Carder

My parents witnessed a terrific thunderstorm on 5th June 1931 when a cloudburst at Spreacombe caused severe flooding in Braunton, Saunton, Croyde, and Georgeham. The floodwater was four feet deep in Croyde and flooded houses on each side of the street to that depth. A pond at Kittiwell, where Millers Brook now stands, burst its banks and added to the devastation. A grass-cutting machine weighing over a ton was swept one hundred and fifty yards from Mill Farm and a wooden footbridge was hurled against the newly built Croyde Bridge which was completely submerged. The parapet of the bridge at Mill Farm weighing about a ton was washed away and carried nearly seventy yards and a pig was washed into the village from a farm over a mile away.

Outside former post office opposite the Manor House Inn.

St. Mary's Road Sweets Cottage

7

St Mary's Road note the high water mark on the old barn wall

Bridge Farm with the flood water starting to recede

At Mr Ellis' butchers shop near Croyde Bridge the water carried joints of meat into the roadway and a number of poultry at the Manor House Inn were drowned. The road from Saunton to Croyde was impassable and hedges were washed clean away. However, Putsborough was virtually untouched and Saunton golf course was undamaged. The water quickly drained away and in 1932 a wall was built at the side of the stream through the village.

My mother at Putsborough with Valerie and me 1936

I was born in The Thatch Cottage at Putsborough on 27th March 1936, the fourth child of Charles and Alice Lewis. My sister Valerie was the eldest, followed by George and Fred. Another sister Margaret, was born after me before we moved to Wee Cott in Croyde, which is now home to Keith and Jennifer Howes, chimney sweeps who have renamed the property 'High Legh'. My sister Joan and brother Tony were born there. My father had bought the field and dug a well, levelled the site, and bought a wooden bungalow with an asbestos roof from Woolaways from its site at Freshwell Field, next to Ruda Caravan Site, formerly Ruda Farm. My father was working at Baggy Farm at the time and Bill Bagster and others helped him to transport the building on a long cart pulled by a horse. They did this on a Sunday, which Bill's father Frank did not approve of as Sunday was a day on which only necessary work such as feeding the animals was undertaken.

As children, we played on Saunton Downs and in the surrounding fields, gathering sticks for the small Dover stove, which was situated in the living room and was our only form of heating and cooking at the time. We had a back kitchen with a sink and one bedroom with a smaller bedroom leading from it; another room could only be entered from outside the property where my older brothers slept.

9

The Lewis Family
My father, Margaret, my mother
George, Fred, me, Valerie outside Wee Cott 1938

Me   and   Margaret
with visitors at Sandbourne Croyde Bay 1946

At the other end of the bungalow was a shed where the dog was housed, along with tools and the explosives which my father used for blasting when digging wells.

The only lighting we had was paraffin lamps and candles and the elsan toilet was situated outside the back door in a small shed. We had one cold tap and no hot water system. In the winter, this pipe would freeze as we were situated on the north side of the hill and we would have to fetch water from the stream, situated further down the lane outside our property.

The well was behind the bungalow and on rare occasions, in very dry weather, the water would cease to flow as the level would fall below the gravity pipe. To re-start the flow we would take cans of water from the stream, unscrew the pipe at the top and pour in the water, which would begin the siphoning.

We had very little coal, all of which had to be carried up from the village. We spent hours on the downs collecting small sticks to get the fire going and large pieces of dead gorse which soon burnt up and gave plenty of heat for the oven. My mother was very superstitious and would never burn dead elderberry branches as she was convinced it would bring us bad luck.

Sunday night was bath night and a galvanised bath was brought in from the shed and placed in front of the fire; water was heated on top of the stove and added to the bath as necessary as we took it in turns to go in the tub.

With my father away some of the time during the war it was very difficult for my mother having to cope with all the washing and cooking with no mod cons that we take for granted today. Carrying food up the lane was a never ending chore and as Wee Cott was north facing the sun only shone on the bungalow for a few months in the summer. She was forever cooking for us, making delicious meals and a variety of cakes and I never remember her complaining. Occasionally we would have roast beef for Sunday lunch and bread and dripping with a sprinkling of salt was a real treat the next day.

At Easter we would collect birds eggs although this is now illegal. When I was young all my friends had egg collections, searching for as many different species as we could find. We also went on the cliffs at Baggy Point, collecting seagulls eggs including those of black backed gulls and if we had surplus eggs we would swop them. During the summer months one of our favourite pastimes was to walk over the downs to a large pond at Saunton Court. There we had found a small boat tied to a tree on the bank which we would row out to the middle of the pond using sticks instead of oars. We had great fun although none of us could swim at that time; we didn`t tell our parents what we were up to as it would have been strictly out of bounds.

We used to look for suitable branches to make stilts, getting our feet jammed in them and often falling off. In the field next to where we lived we tied ropes to overhanging branches and made swings placing a piece of wood at the bottom end to make a seat.

COCK ROCK

Built in 1923 as a summer residence for Miss Girvin, a playright, and Miss Cosens.

It was destroyed by fire in August 1941

© Photograph from the

Tom Bartlett collection

Chapter II   SCHOOL

When I came of school age, I walked with my elder sister and two brothers to Georgeham School, approximately two miles away. Wee Cott is situated half a mile from Cross on the main Croyde to Georgeham road, up an un-made muddy lane. If we had a penny, we could catch the bus at Cross to Georgeham.

During the Second World War, some buses ran on gas. A trailer housing a coal fire was towed behind the bus. This produced gas and pipes connected to the bus carried the fuel to the engine. Sometimes the bus didn't have enough power to ascend Forda Hill, we would lean back at this point, believing this would stop the bus going up the hill! On several occasions we had to walk to school from there. At Georgeham, the terminus, the driver would stoke the boiler for the return journey.

Georgeham School and old school house 2009

The teachers at Georgeham School at that time were Miss Hughes, Mrs Heard and the Headmistress Miss Cann. As we only had an elsan toilet at home, which was commonplace at the time, I had never seen a toilet and cistern before. Consequently the first time I flushed the toilet at school I was so frightened I ran outside as I thought it was going to flood the entire building!

There was a coal boiler in the main room which heated cast iron radiators. Apart from the lucky few who had bikes, or travelled by bus, most of us walked to school so there were plenty of wet coats and shoes to be dried before the journey home.

In the summer, weather permitting, we were taken on nature walks to Pickwell or Putsborough and later, back in the classroom, we had to answer questions on which plants and birds we had seen. Part of the field at the back of the school, called Netherhams, had been used as a playing field but was requisitioned during the war for much needed crops.

Evacuees and childen of families who had moved to the country to escape the city bombing joined us at school.

We had a cooked midday meal and every day we had crates of milk delivered. After the third of a pint bottles had been shared out, any spares were given to children who didn't live on farms presumably because it was reckoned that farmers' families had plenty of milk and cream. Occasionally we slipped out of school to buy sweets at Taylors Stores in the centre of the village. If we had managed to save a few pennies we could buy liquorice pipes and coils, bulls eyes, and sherbert dips, or Horlicks tablets and black imps, neither of which were rationed. A lady who lived at The Barn, near the school, made and sold homemade sweets.

Being a church school every so often the Vicar, Mr Sharples, came to take the service and sometimes we put on plays at the school or the Institute (Georgeham Village Hall) to entertain our parents and other villagers.

Friday afternoons were one of my favourite times because we listened to the radio at school, mainly current affairs and interesting stories. This was a small portable Pye radio which was powered by a dry battery and could be moved to any of the rooms. At home we had a large Bush radio which was kept on a table in the corner of the kitchen this ran off a dry battery which lasted for about six

Forda

©*Photograph from the
Tom Bartlett collection*

Manor House Inn and Croyde Post Office pre1938   R.L.Knight collection

weeks and needed additional power from an accumulator which was a wet battery. We had two of these accumulators, one being used at home and the other which we carried down the lane to Cross where it was collected each week by Chichester's of Braunton for recharging.

On the way home from school we would walk from the first electricity pole, run from the next, walk, and then run. We would also amuse ourselves by throwing small stones onto a galvanised shed at North Hole Farm, thoroughly enjoying the noise it produced! The shed's owner, Farmer Thorne, did not share our opinion and would threaten to call the police

In the summer, if we had a few pennies to spare, we would call at Frog Street Farm to buy Royal Sovereign strawberries or raspberries from Mr and Mrs Lovering. They used to grow them in their garden and the small field opposite. The sweet smell of the harvested fruit in their porch was wonderful.

We also picked wild strawberries on Saunton Down behind Wee Cott. If we managed half a cup, adding a little sugar and the top of the milk was our idea of luxury.

We used to collect our groceries and paraffin from Emily Reed's shop opposite the Manor House Inn, which she ran with her daughter. Emily would usually manage to give us a sweet or a biscuit even though they were rationed.

Each evening we used to collect our milk from Tom Tucker at Hillsnest. He didn't deliver to us at Wee Cott as we were so far from the main road. He would

15

Cross

drive a pony and trap, selling milk in the village. Later he used a van with a tap at the back connected to a churn, which he used to fill peoples` jugs and bowls. Sometimes we had to wait for the milk and Mrs Tucker's mother would give us a slice of home-made fruit cake which was a very welcome treat. Other times I would play with the bantams in their garden. We were always hungry and thirsty and we used to drink some of the milk on the way home and then re-fill the can with water from the pump at Cross. Sometimes, for a treat, mum would put the milk on the stove, then remove it just before it came to the boil, so that we could have the cream with some jam. If this produced no cream, she would grumble about the quality of the milk, although she guessed what we had done! Another 'game' was to swing the can over and over, without the lid coming off. Not a good idea and we got in trouble for that, as we would invariably lose some of the contents.

Mr. and Mrs. Lewis who lived at Cross (no relation to us) would give us a few sweets if we picked a bunch of wild flowers for them, and Bill Miles, then working at Nalgo (now Unison), would get sweets from the stationed Americans for his daughter and give some to us.

As children, in order to have toys, we had to be inventive. We would make tractors, for example, from an empty cotton reel. Mum would be sewing and we wouldn`t leave her alone until she either gave us an empty cotton reel or actually removed the thread from a reel. We would then use a knife to make notches all around the edge of the reel to imitate the tractor wheel treads. Next we'd cut two

16

Corney Lewis and his wife on honeymoon 1906

small sections of candle a quarter inch thick. We would take some spare elastic and thread it through the centre of the reel. Once out the other end, we'd thread on the quarter inch of candle, thread the elastic back through the same hole, making sure to place a matchstick in the elastic loop. At the other end we would substitute the matchstick for a small pencil and wind up the tractor to make it move. It would usually travel for a while.

We were delighted if we managed to get hold of some old pram wheels to make a trolley. Wood, nails and string were in short supply – even used nails would be straightened out. Bumping down the hills and lanes and trying to steer our homemade trolleys resulted in many mishaps.

Nurse Jefferies lived at Cross and had a surgery opposite her house. If we cut ourselves we would be sent down to her but we were afraid of her as she was stern and had no sympathy for us!

Mr. Corney Lewis who lived nearby, at My Rest, Cross was a dentist. We would go to him if we had toothache and he would extract the offending tooth at his home. In 1906 he and his wife were visiting relations in Croyde while on their honeymoon. Riding a Norton motorbike registration BO 152, they were the first to drive a motorised vehicle over the new road from Saunton to Croyde. This road which my Grandfather helped to build was effectively a toll road, a fee of possibly a penny had to be paid, the land belonging to 'Squire' Dennis and Christie Estate.

New road into Croyde showing gates which could be closed or locked 1906

St Mary's Church Croyde

Baptist Chapel at Cross 2009

St.George`s Church Georgeham

I was baptized and confirmed at St.George`s Church Georgeham in 1951

On Sunday mornings we went to Croyde Baptist Chapel at Cross to attend Sunday school. Most of the village children would be there and some of the older ones helped to teach the infants. Miss Nora Cook (now Mrs Isaac of Crowborough Farm) was one of the teachers as well as Queenie Avery (later she married Rupert Colwill), with Mr Holmes as Minister. I remember how kind they all were to us. We had prizes for good attendance and all enjoyed the Sunday school outings during the year,which usually included a meal. As children we didn't go far from Croyde but I remember once going on a Sunday school outing to Westward Ho! It seemed such a long journey; I was convinced we had gone to a foreign country! Mr Holmes doubled as a barber, cutting our hair in a wooden hut in his garden.

During the war, there was a truck parked in a field above Wee Cott. This was a Royal Air Force military vehicle, manned part-time. It was used for filling in logbooks and communications and we used to look in the window at the books and telephone inside. We all carried gas masks and these were obtained and serviced at Forda Farm by Mr. Silvester. Childrens' gas masks were called 'Mickey Mouse' as the tongue at the front flipped up and down as we breathed. Orange juice, cod liver oil and malt for children were available from Chapel Farm.

When we heard a German plane approaching the area, my mother would tell us to shelter underneath the kitchen table. All the windows were blacked out at night and there were wardens in the village checking for glimmers of light. Lights on bicycles had a visor covering them so that the light only shone downwards. Rabbiting at night with torches was suspended.

During and after the war, the May family farmed the large fields on Saunton Down. When they cut the corn we would follow the binder and run after the rabbits, helping to catch them. After work, the rabbits caught were distributed; the farmer would have most of them, some would go to the farm-workers and, if we were lucky, we might receive one. This was either taken home for a meal or sold for one shilling which was our pocket money. We were very disappointed if a field was cut over two days, as the rabbits would have time to escape!

Heathercombe Hotel overlooking Putsborough Beach was taken over by London County Council and used as a boarding school for girl evacuees during the war. The building was constructed of wood and essex board and parts of it were of asbestos. In 1941 a fire occurred and the children were led to safety but unfortunately a woman helper, Mrs Muriel Sweet, died in the blaze. The firemen were on duty for twenty four hours and although unable to save the cliffside building, they were able to prevent an extensive gorse fire.

Nearby **Casa del Mare** was built before the Second World War by Mr. Chivers and run as a guest house. Boy evacuees were housed and taught there during the war. They left and eventually Mr.Chivers sold the building. It was re-named Putsborough Sands Hotel and changed hands several times before being demolished. Clifton Court now stands on the site. Some evacuees stayed with families

Heathercombe Hotel c1935

Casa del Mare (far right)   Heathercombe Hotel (top middle) c1938

21

in the area. I was friendly with some boys from Croydon who came back here to see me several years later.

In 1947 we had several weeks of very heavy snow and frost and we could not get to school either by bus or on foot, so we made sledges from sheets of old galvanised iron. We used to sledge in Tom Parsons field near Robbers Hall during the day and on moon-lit nights. When the sled run was compacted and icy, it became so slippery we were unable to stop and we went straight through the hedge and into the lane. Heaps of frozen dung under the snow in the field also added to the excitement, making for a bumpy ride! We had very little warm clothing, no gloves and shoes that frequently had holes. The soles were mended each evening with cardboard from the boxes used to carry the groceries up to the bungalow – an early form of recycling!

The Allen family, who lived next to Robbers Hall, had children of our age and they would allow us into their cottage to defrost. Clothes and shoes were rationed and we relied on hand-me-downs, whether they fitted or not. I can remember once, after the war, I had a new pair of boots and I had to stand on newspaper to try them on.

Robbers Hall at Cross   © *Photograph from the*
Tom Bartlett collection

Chapter III
AMERICAN FORCES AND HOME GUARD

During the latter part of World War II, the American forces took over Nalgo (Unison). They were billeted in Nissan huts, which were galvanised semi-circular huts with concrete slabs on the floor and a stove with a fire in the centre. These huts were auctioned at the end of the war and were bought by farmers, smallholders and pig farmers for use as stock pens.

N.A.L.G.O Holiday Centre 1950
Two Nissan huts are still evident to the right of Nalgo

Ora Stone was originally an agricultural field. The Americans took it over, took down the road hedge and concreted the entire entrance to a depth of several metres. At the top of the field, which is now chalet bungalows, there was a large metal shed where they kept smaller machinery and carried out repairs. This shed was later sold to Maldram and Jones, corn and seed merchants of Barnstaple. The rest of the field was covered in chippings and was used for the storage of larger equipment: tanks, Dukws, lorries, caterpillars, etc. It was quite normal to see tanks, jeeps and amphibious vehicles rumbling through Croyde and large groups of American troops in the village. As children, we were always glad to see them as they always had plenty of sweets, chewing gum and doughnuts. As they drove past, we would shout "Got any gum, chum?" Sometimes they would throw candy to us, with the inevitable reply, "Got any sisters, mister?" As ration books limited us to a small amount of sweets every month, any extra was welcome! It fascinated us children to see them climbing the telegraph poles wearing spiked boots, to wire for communications.

23

American Dukws passing the Carpenters Arms c1943/4

During the warmer months, they dammed Croyde stream where it entered the beach, then washed in the water. They often left their soap on the banks and we were delighted to find such a scarce commodity to take home. Some of the troops would ride their motorbikes or jeeps around the lanes, even getting as far as Wee Cott. My father, who was often catching rabbits, must have told them how much we enjoyed a meal of rabbit and potatoes. On one occasion I can remember my mother giving some of the Americans a large dish containing a freshly roasted rabbit surrounded by roast potatoes.

Sometimes they would hold dances or other social activities at Nalgo and invite the villagers. Foreign prisoners were transported in lorries and dropped off at various farms in Croyde and the surrounding area to work during the day. Some were reluctant to work, whilst others enjoyed the outdoor life. If a farmer couldn't get on with a certain prisoner, he would ask for another. The prisoners were collected each evening and taken back to their camp.

The Home Guard at Croyde consisted of men living locally and from a variety of occupations including farmers, farm workers, gardeners, drivers and office workers. (not all the members of Croyde Home Guard are in the picture opposite) Mr Simons was the officer in charge and the men trained at Nalgo under the watchful eye of Sergeant Major Pedrick. As well as drills and manoeuvres he taught them to clean their Canadian Ross rifles and clean and strip down their Lewis guns. If they didn't get it right they had to stay until the weapon was correctly assembled. They took part in sentry duties and map reading. The Army

Home Guard c1942
L-R   Ern Lang, Fred Baldwin, Bill Tanner, Walter Ley, Jo Fletcher, Fred Manning
Tom Lang, Bill Bagster, Hector Fowler, Charlie Lang.
Outside Georgeham Institute

instructed them in weapon training. The men were also taken on a private coach to Saunton Burrows where they trained at the firing range using 14lb and 20lb. Blacker Bombard spigot mortars, firing at an old tank as a target. Later, this range was used by the American troops.

At the cliffs underneath Saunton Sands Hotel they practised running up to an imaginary tank- a sheet of metal- and attaching a sticky bomb, then making a cautious retreat. At Downend side of Croyde Beach they used live hand grenades, throwing them behind the rocks. Once the pin was removed it was seven seconds before it exploded.

The men also trained with Woolacombe Commandos using thunder flashes on manoeuvres to simulate hand grenades and were shown films at a cinema in Ilfracombe to improve their training. They practised at a quarry at Forda using 9mm sub machine sten guns and at Boode, near Braunton there was a firing range where they fired at targets, measuring 200 and 400 yards, the range is still there, now derelict of course. With all this training going on there were bound to be some amusing tales in the area. Gilbert Gammon didn`t have a large enough uniform so used to wear his best blue suit to practices until a new uniform was provided. Tom Lang had to wait for a pair of size twelve boots.

25

Some of the Home Guard trained with broom handles or pitch forks until they were issued with weapons. The Vicar was given a sledgehammer to smash the petrol pumps outside the Kings Arms if Georgeham was invaded. In 1941 there was a scare in the village that an invasion was imminent.

Sandy Lane Woolacombe, similar scenes found in Croyde 1943/4

American Jeep 1943/4

Photograph taken just hours before the fire broke out

The Nalgo Holiday Camp re-opened in May 1947 with over two hundred visitors, and the occasion was celebrated with a dance in the main dance hall. Some two hours after it had finished the hall was a blazing inferno, by 9.30 am the next morning it had been completely destroyed. Damage was estimated at several thousand pounds.

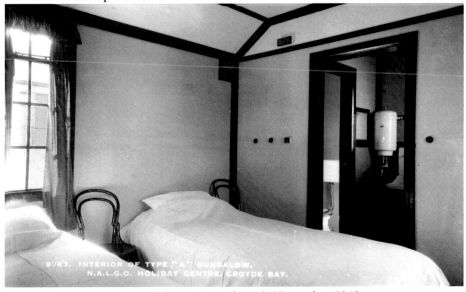

N.A.L.G.O   interior of type 'A' Bungalow 1945

Cecil Parsons Cpl Merlin A. Murphy, U.S Forces, Myra Parsons. December 1943

This is a photograph of Cecil and Myra Parsons with Cpl. Merlin A. Murphy who was billeted at Nalgo with the American forces preparing for D.Day. Merlin had a lovely tenor singing voice and Cecil used to play the piano for him to keep up his singing practice. Merlin also sang a few solos at the local chapel.

Originally called the Rhapsody Makers, the Croydolians were a local band who played at the Institute, Georgeham and at the clubroom in Croyde for dances and social events. Mrs Fanny Barton, who also taught music at home, played the piano, with John Crawley on the drums and Cecil and his mother Cordelia Parsons, playing piano accordions, also taking over the other instruments if required, with other local people helping out when necessary. At the Institute the band was seated on trestles at one end of the hall, but with no microphone and the sound of feet dancing on the floor, it was difficult to hear the music at the far end of the room! The band members were taken to Georgeham by Alf Reed who put the drums on the dickey seat at the back of his car. If this transport was not available they travelled by bus and then had a lift back in Arthur Brown`s car. There was a collection at the dances and after paying for the venue the band shared any extra, sometimes only amounting to a few shillings. When the American forces attended the dances it usually resulted in a generous amount of money.

Chapter IV   WORK

From the age of seven (1943), I used to deliver Sunday papers for Charlie Waldron. Charlie worked for Stan Simmonds, corn merchants of Braunton during the week and on Sundays he brought the papers to Croyde in their lorry.

I helped Frank Tucker at Manor Farm, Putsborough, to bag potatoes stored in the barn. I also helped him collect the money at the car park for Putsborough Beach. At that time the car park entrance was opposite the private road at Vention. He had a pony and trap and used to let the horse out in the field to graze while he was at the car park. As well as the parking money he used to cadge the odd cigarette from visitors! Frank Tucker was retired and lived with his wife and daughter Audrey in Croyde, while his son, Stanley, was farming at Manor Farm.

Me at Combas farm

When I was eleven I worked at weekends and holidays for Alf Tucker at Combas Farm. When I was thirteen I left Wee Cott and went to live with Alf, his wife Elizabeth and their daughter Ethel and went to school from there. Bill Shapland lived at Tuckers Farm, Putsborough, now known as Putsborough Court, we would meet and catch the bus on Croyde Bridge to go to Braunton Secondary Modern School. During the holidays, Alf paid me £1 per week for a six day working week. He was in very poor health and glad to have me there on hand to help him. For me it was luxury to have my own bedroom, plenty of home produced meat, eggs, cream and even a flush toilet!

Corn, potatoes, mangolds, turnips and swedes were grown on the farm and the livestock consisted of Devon cattle, approximately sixty sheep and two cart horses called Lion and Duke. I was small for my age, only five feet tall and weighing about six stone and I used to groom these horses and harness them ready for work. This wasn't easy, as they were much taller than I was, but thankfully they were good-natured and stood patiently while I stretched under their bellies to fasten the chains and girth if needed. Both horses were required for most jobs on the farm, such as harrowing or rolling heavy ground, operating a grass machine, a binder for cutting corn or pulling a corn drill or simply ploughing. For the lighter jobs, such as rolling down corn or chain harrowing, only one horse was needed. Lion was generally used to pull a cart or a tipping butt; the latter used for swedes and mangolds or transporting farmyard manure from the dung heap to the fields. Every few months, I rode Lion to Braunton in order to have him shod, the nearest blacksmith being Mr. Gliddon in North Street. Duke was never shod and only used for fieldwork.

Every Saturday I would take the horse and cart and collect the week's groceries from Sweets Cottage where Sam Hernaman lived. These provisions were ordered and sent out by carrier from Barnstaple. Two carriers I remember went by the names of Sexon and Prouse.

Braunton Park 1949
Judges unknown
L-R Boys: unknown, Ronnie Bates, me , Mervyn Norman, unknown

At shearing time, Ronnie Bates, Mervyn Norman, Robert Hancock and I would visit various farms in the area to practise hand shearing. We had to use both hands to get even stripes on the sheep's back left and right, and competitions were held at Braunton Park for the best shorn sheep.

Sometimes we would get together and cycle to Woolacombe or Ilfracombe or on occasion to Arlington Court as a change from work. Another treat, usually during a winter evening, was to catch a bus to Braunton (seven pence return) and watch a film at the Plaza (now John Patt's fruit shop).

I can remember seeing the author Henry Williamson many times around the village. On one particular occasion when I was eleven years old I was walking up the narrow track from Vention Cottage, Putsborough on my way back to Combas Farm. Henry Williamson accompanied by two teenage boys, was walking down the lane towards me. He was tall and I thought rather scary looking. When we met they blocked my way and as a joke Henry Williamson waved his arms at me and laughed. I was really frightened and squeezed past them, running as fast as I could up the hill.

Henry Williamson on the cliff path to Baggy Point overlooking Putsborough Beach. early 1920s. Courtesy of the Henry Williamson Literary Estate.

I can also remember seeing Negley Farson a well known author who lived at The Grey House, Vention, bumping down Combas Lane in an old Ford car on the way to the Manor House Inn. I was told that when he needed inspiration for a book he would have a drinking session and heated discussion with some of the locals and boasted about his grandfather General Negley who served in the American Civil War. After several hours his wife would collect him and take him home.

Their son Daniel was also an author and a colourful character around Croyde who lived for many years at Vention in the house left to him by his parents.

Negley and Eve Farson in the grounds of The Grey House c1950
taken from the book , The World of Negley Farson by Daniel Farson

My Father used to tell me about John 'Muggy' Smith a real old character who lived in a shack part way up Cloutmans Lane. Henry Williamson was friendly with Muggy and wrote about him in his books.

John 'Muggy' Smith outside his shack in Cloutmans Lane. c1925
He died in 1929 aged 75
Taken by Henry Williamson. Courtesy of the Henry Williamson Literary Estate

Haymaking at Combas Farm

To obtain the best hay with the highest protein, we would cut the grass in June, and would turn it every day with pitchforks until it was dry and ready to be collected by horse and cart and made into a rick. Depending on the acreage, we would mark out an oblong approximately four by eight paces and make a raised bed of brambles, bushes and branches. This formed a base and kept the hay off the ground. The stack was made in the traditional shape and allowed to settle before being thatched with wheat reed to keep it dry. Sometimes a rick would settle unevenly and lean sideways and props were needed to stop the rick from falling. If too many props were needed, other farmers would joke "Is that rick running away?"

Thatched ricks at Combas farm   c1960

On the ridge of the rick, bundles of straw would be laid end to end. These were tied with straw rope and speared. The rick was then thatched, starting at the bottom of the apex, placing the first layer with the butts downward, then another layer. This continued until the top was reached. The last layer would be reversed with the butts upward. As the thatching advanced, each layer would be speared and tied with rope approximately one foot apart. The spears were driven in at an angle so that the rain would run off them and not into the rick.

I remember a neighbouring farmer carrying his hay too quickly and making a large rick. As a result the grass overheated causing internal combustion. Three chimneys had to be cut into the rick using hay knives in order to let the heat out and prevent a fire. When hay was needed in the winter, we would remove a portion of reed and cut the required amount with a hay knife.

Harvesting

The crops were cut with a binder in July and August. Six sheaves were grouped together to form a stook (known locally as a stack) and these stooks were generally left in the field to dry out for up to three weeks for oats and one week for barley, to make sure all the sap was out of the joints in the stems. A base was made to keep the sheaves off the ground, similar to those prepared for a hay rick. The first layer of sheaves was started in the middle with the sheaves stacked up then we gradually worked towards the edge getting flatter on the way out. The heads of corn would be resting on the previous sheaf. In this way, a rick was made keeping the middle full all of the time. As we got to the top, each sheaf was placed slightly inwards to give a slanting apex appearance. I would use a large wooden rake to collect all the loose straw left in the field and this was placed on top of the rick to make a smooth surface before it was thatched in a similar way to the hay rick.

Harvesting at Downend 1930s
Boy unknown William Parsons and Bob Fowler of Mill Farm

Stooks (known locally as stacks) of corn at Downend   1930s

Carrying corn at Downend   1930s

Threshing

Threshing generally took place in the winter months when all the spears, rope and reed would be carefully removed from the rick and stored in a loft to be hopefully used again.

Most farmers hired a steam engine and thresher. In my younger days, it was hired from Bill Isaac's yard in Wrafton. Bill was accompanied by Albert Mock or Fred Manning. The threshing machine was usually brought in the day before and levelled using blocks if necessary. The steam engine had to be aligned exactly so that there was no danger that the big drive belt to the thresher would fly off at speed, as there were no belt guards. In the morning we collected dry sticks to light the fire in the firebox of the steam engine. Once alight, steam coal was used to keep it going. Two or three men pitched the sheaves from the rick onto the thresher board. One man would cut the binder twine on each sheaf. The key man was the one who fed the corn into the 'fly' (a rotating metal drum) because if it wasn't done carefully and steadily, making sure all the binder twine was cut, this could throw the belts off and everything would grind to a halt. One man would make sure the grain was continually bagged by pulling a lever that closed one shoot and opened another, to start filling an empty sack. One bag collected the small grain. Another man would weigh and tie each sack and wheel it away. If the corn was being sold, it would go into hired 'West of England' sacks: barley in 2cwt and oats in 1.5cwt. Once the corn was removed, the straw would be taken along the straw walkers to the back end of the thresher where it would be bundled up into wads of straw tied with two lengths of binder twine. Another rick was made with these wads, then thatched and used for stock feeding and bedding.

The worst job to have during threshing was to clean the rubbish or 'douse', as we called it, from under the straw walker. This was where every boy started. Worst of all was barley; the barley ears got inside clothes and the dust into eyes that were still red and sore the next morning. The 'douse' from the oats was stored, then mixed with good oats and given to the horses. This made the horses chew their food, which was better for their digestion. If wheat was being threshed and the straw was being kept for thatching, a reed comber was used. This was similar to the process for making wads of straw, except the straw came out loose on two big metal arms. It was then manually tied into bundles, or a 'nitch', as we called it, and stacked in a heap until needed or sold for thatching homes or ricks. Ten or eleven men were needed when threshing, so farmers and farm-workers helped each other and in the middle of the day everyone would be invited into the farmhouse for a well-deserved roast dinner.

After a few years, Stanley Tucker of Manor Farm Putsborough bought a thresher and took over some of the threshing in Croyde, including at Combas Farm.

During the summer months, after finishing work for Alf, I would go to the allotments on the Putsborough road and help George Green. He rented several acres from the council and grew potatoes, cauliflowers, savoys and cabbage.

Barley threshing at Ash Barton Farm Sept 1949. Tenant farmer H.J. Bowden
William Isaac 3rd from right.
This type of thresher was used around Croyde farms

To supplement my income further, I used to catch moles. I would skin them and nail the skins on the back of the barn door to dry, then send them to a tannery. I received eleven pence for each skin. Alf and Gilbert Gammon at Myrtle Farm paid me a shilling per mole for each one I caught on their land. Due to the declining numbers, I was paid two shillings per mole in subsequent years. There was also a demand for stoat, weasel, badger and fox skins.

I had a small piece of garden at Combas Farm in which I grew vegetables and sold them to the village shops. I also kept a few chickens and sold the eggs to Fred Brown who served in the butchers shop in Croyde. Another profitable sideline was the sale of rabbits. Using my two ferrets, Ronnie Bates and I spent many a weekend catching rabbits. Alternatively we would catch them at night using a dog and a torch or shoot them during daylight hours in the summer months. We gutted and cleaned them and left them in pairs in a shed behind the Manor House Inn where a Mr Gammon collected them and paid two to three shillings for each one. Several other local trappers used this service.

There was no electricity nor telephone line at Combas Farm, a traditional Devon longhouse, so we used candles and paraffin lamps for lighting.

There was a bodley for cooking and an open grate in the sitting room, which was lit in the winter. In the kitchen there was a big open fire with a pot-hook above it. Water was hand-pumped from a well and beside the pump there was a brick furnace, which was used when a large amount of hot water was needed, such as on wash days or when a pig was slaughtered. The water was heated by a wood fire situated directly underneath the copper boiler.

Although Mrs. Tucker unfortunately died soon after I went to live there, Ethel continued to accommodate visitors in the summer months. Water was heated on the bodley and taken upstairs to the visitors, who used jugs and basins in their bedrooms. Alf wouldn't change his clocks in spring and autumn, so we had summer all year round! This caused some amusement to the neighbouring farms as we had different lunchtimes and was known locally as Combas time! After Alf died in 1954, the house and land was rented by John and Gwen Adams who still farm there today.

John and Gwen Adams cutting oats on Ora Hill c1958

John Adams told me an extraordinary tale about a rat, or rather a couple of rats, which he witnessed at Woodstock on the Putsborough road. He saw a rat on its back holding a hen's egg between its front legs. This rat was being pulled across the road towards a corn rick by its tail by another rat. There was another farmer who witnessed a similar scene in Georgeham this time rats moving a whole nest of eggs in a similar way. Fact, not fiction!

I met my wife Shirley at Combas Farm in 1963 when she came to work there from Chelmsford, Essex, helping Gwen with the summer visitors. We were married at Georgeham Parish Church in 1964. Our daughter Maria was born in 1968 and Caroline four years later.

View from Ora with John Adams' sheep c1960

Chapter V
CROYDE SHOPS & PUBLIC HOUSES

There used to be a **butchers shop** at the end of Bridge Farm, by the side entrance, run by Tommy Ellis. Later a butchers shop was built on the opposite side of the road where the notice-board for Croyde Village Hall now stands. Tommy Ellis opened two or three times a week and people queued on the road waiting to be served. This was only a temporary building and was later demolished. Across the other side of the stream were two cottages; the first one was turned into a butchers shop and run by the Ellis family for several years. It is now Blue Groove. Next door was Ann Gray's dress shop for many years, it changed hands several times and for a short time was a chemist shop. It is now Redwood surf shop.

Tommy Ellis Butchers L/H side of bridge 1930s

My grandfather had a timber-framed shop erected opposite the Thatch for butcher Arty Thomas to rent. It was later taken over by Bob Causey and then Robert Withecombe. In 1980 I acquired it, demolished it, then had it rebuilt as it is today. For a few years we ran it as a greengrocery then sold it. It was turned into a surf shop, as it remains today.

Ted and Joan Butler bought the **General Stores** opposite the Manor House Inn in 1946 from Joyce and Emily Reed. Ted ran the general store and Joan converted the former post office and exchange into a **drapery** store. Mr and Mrs Sanderson had taken over the running of the post office in 1938 when it was transferred to May Cottage.

Webbers Stores, another general store selling food, provisions, paraffin, candles, papers, etc. was owned and run by Mr and Mrs Webber, their daughters

41

Webbers Stores c1958

May and Mary and sons Frank and Jack. Later, May and her husband and family took over the running of the shop. It was then acquired by Mr and Mrs Clough Wilson, then by Bernard and Barbara Maskell who converted it into a restaurant and ice cream parlour known as Aunt Sally's. It changed hands again and is now known as Hobbs Restaurant and ice cream parlour.

Next to Webbers Stores was a cottage now known as the **Old Cream Shop** which Mr and Mrs Lock and family changed into a cake shop, also selling confectionary and ice cream. It changed hands several times, becoming famous for selling clotted cream and ice cream, and now also sells surfing equipment and provides tuition. Beside the Old Cream Shop was another cottage. Ted and Joan Butler moved there in 1965 from opposite the Manor House Inn and converted the downstairs rooms into a general store and drapery. Betty and Roy Fairweather bought it in 1972 and converted it into **Croyde Gem, Rock and Shell Museum**, and a gift shop which they ran with son Ian for thirty two years. It is now a surf shop. Stephanie Cole, the actress, lived here when she was young and used to visit my mother when she came back to Croyde on holiday.

The original **Brook Stores** was a small chalet type building situated on the site of the present shop, run by William (Pop) Parsons, his wife Cordelia, son Cecil and daughter Myra. In 1948 they took over the running of the post office from Mr and Mrs Sanderson and ran this in conjunction with the general store.

There was another building situated on the site of the current post office with tables and chairs outside, where cream teas for one shilling and snacks were served. This was the only canteen privately run in North Devon during the Second World War for servicemen. A local committee collected funds to run it, local

Looking down Hobbs Hill c1920

Brook Stores and Tea Garden owned by the Parsons Family 1935. R.L.Knight

Brook House Tea Garden 1935 R.L.Knight Collection

Cecil Parsons with British soldiers in Brook House Tea Gardens 1940

British Regiments were stationed at Nalgo, with the Berkshire Regiment being the last prior to the American forces arrival.

farmers supplied the milk and ladies living locally served the teas. The service-men could relax by playing darts, write letters home on notepaper provided free of charge or play the piano or numerous games provided.

Helped by Nora, who lived with the family, Cordelia kept many animals including goats, rabbits, pigs, dogs and a pet lamb. She was often to be seen taking the goats and dogs up the lanes where the goats would feed on the hedgerows. They also had tortoises, bought from Woolworths for sixpence and are now over seventy years old. Pop used to make ice cream from goats milk and sell it from the back of Brook House, two pence wafers being the cheapest.

He also trained as a tailor and was known as `Tailor Bill`. The family lived in Brook House which was thatched until it was destroyed by fire in 1960 and the roof was replaced by asbestos tiles. When the tearoom was demolished the new post office was built and transferred from Brook Stores. Cecil ran the post office until he retired and Mark Atkins took over. It is now run by Mary and John Corry. In the meantime Brook Stores was taken over by Dave and Audrey Twitchen and sons and is now run by David and Daphne Johnson and their son Dan. Cecil sold Brook Stores, the post office and Brook House in 2005 and moved to Georgeham. He continues to play the organ at Georgeham Church.

Joy Young ran a clothes shop at **May Cottage**, then it was converted into a tea shop. It is now a private residence, as is Croyde Weavers, the former gift shop next door. The property opposite the Manor House Inn, vacated by Ted and Joan Butler, was run as a restaurant and changed hands several times. This, together with the clubroom, has now been converted into living accommodation.

St.Mary's Road early1950s
L-R Brook House, Croyde Weavers and May Cottage

Brook House 1934
Mrs Cordelia Parsons,   unknown , Mr William 'Pop'Parsons
Cecil Parsons   Myra Parsons   Snooker the Dog

Brook House fire 1960

The **Little Pink Shop** in Moor Lane was originally owned by Carrie and Harry Fowler. They opened it in the 1920s and sold fruit and vegetables most of which Harry grew in the adjoining field. They sold the shop to Mr Lock in 1950 and it changed hands several times and is now a surf shop owned and run by Steve Thomas.

George Symons bought **Ora Stone Field** in 1948 and with his wife Alice developed a caravan site and ran a general store. Later, it was taken over by their daughter Marcia and her husband, David Maddocks. It is now a cul-de-sac of houses named Ora Stone Park.

George and Alice Symons
outside the tea shop at Downend carpark. c1946

Orastone Caravan Site 1980

Opposite the former **Police House** (now a private residence next to 'The Thatch') were garages run by Alf Reed. He used to charge batteries, keep spare parts and repair bikes and also ran a taxi business. The premises were taken over by Gordon Hernaman for agricultural engineering. Later, the garages were demolished and Honey Cott and Dove Cottage were built on the site.

When we had a village policeman, living opposite, he used to rent one garage and keep his bike and car in there. I remember one policeman in particular called Charlie Morris, who used to keep his Ford Prefect there, registration number FUO 355. At that time we used to congregate on Croyde Bridge, playing football and maybe being a nuisance and Charlie Morris would appear and say, "Right! Pack-up your circus and get off home!"... and we did! Sometimes we would climb the huge elm trees; there were a lot of them in the village before Dutch Elm disease arrived and Charlie Morris would say, "I can't see you but I know you're up there!"

There was no wall beside the Catholic Church (opposite Brook House) as there is today, so we would cycle down beside the bridge, along Croyde Stream and out into Watery Lane, playing tick. Cattle could also walk in from there and drink from the stream.

There were petrol pumps at **Brier House**, next to the Manor House Inn, run by Mr. and Mrs. Dolimore. They were taken over by John Lippiatt, who also owned a coach which was used for outings from the village, being driven by John Lippiatt or Jack Boucher. Mr. and Mrs. Reg Summers opened a garage and repair shop there and continued selling petrol for many years before moving to the present site of Croyde Motors in the village.

Brier House with petrol pumps

Home House c1952

Albert Treasure took over the garage at Brier House before moving to Newberry Garage in Georgeham. There was also an old-fashioned pump at **Home House**, run by Kathleen and Edgar White. The petrol was pumped up by hand into a round glass container which measured the amount of fuel being transferred to the vehicle. They also sold oil, paraffin, car accessories and provided a taxi service.

I remember Mr. and Mrs. Warren and their sons living at the **Thatched Barn**, where they ran a tea shop and sold gifts. Miss Chivers bought the property and ran the restaurant and served evening meals. When Bernard and Barbara Maskell acquired the Thatched Barn they made many alterations and opened it as a public house. It is now owned by Eddie, Terry, and Rocky who continue to run The Thatch as a well-known pub and restaurant, in addition to Billy Budds which they acquired in 2000 and the Priory opposite which they bought from Christine Mitchell in 2007.

The Thatched Barn
As a tea shop and art and craft centre 1950

The Carpenters Arms was run by Charlie (Slogger) Brown during the war. For many years afterwards it was run by the Court family, firstly Bert and Win then by their son, Les and his wife Sheila. It changed hands several times and was renamed **Billy Budds,** after a local carpenter who lived at Meadow Cottage on the footpath to the beach. He was known as Gunner Budd because as a coastguard he fired the rocket, attaching a rope to stricken ships to rescue the crews. He was also an undertaker, making the coffins in his workshop next door, and he also cut our hair on Sunday mornings! He smoked woodbines which could be bought in a paper packet of five. He was short and stocky and breathless, and while cutting our hair, he would blow ash over us and nip our ears!

Hobbs Hill with The Carpenters Arms at the top   *R.L.Knight*

The **Manor House Inn** was run by Mrs Treasure, a very large and generous lady, and her daughter Serena. When the war finished, her son Fred came home and took over. It has changed hands many times since, and now has a large restaurant as well as the public bars.

Manor House Inn

Before mains water was brought to Croyde, there were many wells in the parish. I can remember water pumps at Cross, Kittiwell, Cott Lane and Watery Lane, amongst others. The well from the Dennis' Estate near Forda supplied some of the homes in the village. Some houses had their own wells. There is a field at Croyde Bay where water is still pumped from a well for horses. We rent this field and maintain the pump. Mains water was brought to Croyde in 1950 by a firm called Quick, Boyde and Kater. The water was pumped from Braunton to a holding tank near Oxford Cross (now known as Ox's Cross) to supply the parish. In 1951 the main sewer was laid by James Dennis and Sons, of Knowle, and the public toilets and council houses were built soon after.

Nowadays we are all used to seeing our refuse collected in large, purpose built vehicles, but the earlier collections were undertaken by Tom Physick using his horse and cart.

Tom Physick (3rd from the right) with his horse and cart helping in the clean up at Georgeham after the flood in June 1931. Robert Brown far right.

Tom Physick c1947

Croyde Post Office, Croyde Club and Social Room opposite Manor House Inn.
R.L.Knight

Before the present **Village Hall** was built, the clubroom above the garage opposite the Manor House Inn was used for many village functions including snooker, billiards, darts, whist drives and skittles. One of the skittles competitions was held over three nights and first prize was an eight-week-old pig donated by the Gammons of Myrtle Farm. My father won it on one occasion. Voting, dances and concerts were held there and many functions were held to raise funds for the building of the present village hall. When dances were held, props were placed in the garage beneath, to strengthen the floor.

The Dennis family who owned several farms in Croyde and Croyde Manor where Mrs Killard-Leavey was born, gave the land on which the new village hall was to be built. On VE night there were celebrations on Croyde Bridge with dancing and singing well into the night. Cecil Parsons played his accordion and money was collected to build the village hall. To raise further funds a fete was held annually in the two fields beside the footpath to the beach. The field to the left contained a skittle alley, sideshows and darts. One tent was supervised by Bill Thomas, who charged members of the public to 'see Ivy in the bath' – and it was just that, a length of ivy floating in a bath of water! On the other side of the footpath the field was roped off to provide running tracks for competitive sports.

Mrs Killard-Leavey, Mrs K.L as she was affectionately known, was a very well- known character involved in many activities and charities including -

Cecil Parsons in 1984 with accordion he played on V E Night

Croyde Manor 2002

CARA (Croyde Area Residents Association) RNLI and Boy Scouts to name but a few. She was also well-known for lobster fishing near her house at Oyster Falls, Downend.

For many years, a religious group known as the House of Faith used to stay in Croyde for two weeks towards the end of the summer. They slept in various guesthouses in the village and cooked their own meals, buying their meat, vegetables and provisions locally. Two or three of them would do the cooking and they ate communally in the clubroom. They used to sit together on the beach, returning to the village for their meals.

Another regular visitor to Croyde was the Boys Brigade who camped at Shadwell, Cott Lane for many years. They had a band and used to march through the village playing their instruments while police controlled the traffic, on their way to the Sunday service at the chapel at Cross.

Maurice Chevalier was also a regular visitor to Croyde in the 1930s.

Boys Brigade on Croyde Bridge c1980

The Dulverton West Hunt outside Bridge Farm. Master Mrs Smythe nee Dennis on 3rd horse from right. My father far right, behind him Arthur and May Brown with Susan in the pram . 1946

Chapter VI   CROYDE FARMS

When I was young there were a lot of working farms in Croyde. Some of them consisted of a few acres of poor ground on which the farmer and his wife struggled to make a living while other farms were larger with more productive land.

Croyde Farm is situated in St. Mary's Road, next to Home House. Mr. and Mrs. Shapland and their children Valerie, Vera, Frederick and John lived there and farmed the land. They later moved to South Hole Farm at Forda and Croyde Farm was taken over by Aubrey and Molly Hernaman with their children Margaret, Derek and John. Aubrey had a mixed farm, a dairy herd and a riding school. There was a cider press in one of the farm buildings on the other side of the road. When there was a good crop and not all the apples were needed for cooking or storage the surplus, and windfalls, were used for cider making. On one occasion I helped Aubrey place the apples under the press and I was given a bottle of cider when it was ready. The farm has now gone back to the Dennis Estate.

Aubrey Hernaman with his cows outside Parminter c1963

Parminter Farm, opposite Home House, was farmed by Stafford Zeale, then taken over by his sons, firstly Dick then Walter Zeale. Walter sold Parminter and built a new house and buildings on his land facing Moor Lane. He called it Cherry Tree Farm and farmed it with his son David. They grew mainly vegetables and potatoes. Later he moved to a larger farm at Willingcott Bridge and sold Cherry Tree Farm to Geoff Lang. This has now become a private house and Geoff transferred the name Cherry Tree to his present farm at Broadway Lane.

Montague Farm L/H and Burrows Farm R/H looking up Watery Lane 1920s

Montague Farm, at the corner of Watery Lane, was farmed by Fred Gammon who used the barn and out-buildings. The house was let separately at the time. He had land in various parts of the village and grew potatoes and vegetables.

Montague Farm (right) with Jack Boucher in Watery Lane c1940   R.L.Knight

Burrows Farm, part of the Incledon-Webber Estate, was farmed by John Lang, his wife Alice and boys, Tom and Geoff. There was a farmhouse and an adjoining cottage which backed onto Watery Lane. The village pound was situated in their yard near Croyde Bridge. Stray stock was kept here until the owner reclaimed them and paid for their keep. When the family moved out, Colonel Webber sold the farmhouse and the cottage. The rick yard, which stretched all the way up Watery Lane and opposite Billy Budds, was sold for building sites. The Lang family was one of the first in the area to have a Ferguson tractor. Tom moved to Lane Head Farm on Putsborough road.

Geoff Lang at Burrows Farm beside the whale bone arch c1934

Burrows Farm c1940
Tom Lang, David Stokes, Aubrey Hernaman
Ken Dawes, Gilbert Kelland

Burrows Farm c1931
Geoff Lang , his mother Alice, Annie Barnes

Geoff Lang, John Lang, Tom Lang, Annie Barnes, John Howard c1950

Chuggs Farm, in Cloutman's Lane was home to Ern Lang and his wife. They had a mixed farm and two carthorses. Ern had a large white hairy dog called Laddie. When we were threshing and rats escaped from the rick Laddie would catch and eat the first half dozen to fill himself up. The farmhouse is now divided into cottages.

Ern Lang c1967

Tom Parsons 1952

Bay View Farm. Ploughing match c1920

George and Neill Hakin rounding up their cattle for the last time at Bay View Farm, after their escape from a field at Combas Lane. They were off to market the next day. c1978

Home Farm 1970

Home Farm, in Cloutmans Lane was owned by the Dennis Estate and farmed by Donald Hernaman, his wife and sons Aubrey and Gordon. They had working horses and a Bristol caterpillar tractor, and later an Alice Chalmer tractor. When Donald and his wife retired to Braunton, the farmhouse deteriorated and parts of it collapsed as it was built of cob and thatch. The Dennis Estate later sold the remains of the farmhouse, outbuildings and several acres of land to Geoff Ward. The site was passed for building consent and is now known as Home Farm Close.

Cott Farm in Cott Lane was owned by Johnnie, Billy and Hetti Webb. They lived in the farmhouse now called 'The Cottage'. Their yard and farm buildings were on the opposite side of the road, and as children, we used to play in a horse-drawn carriage that was no longer used. They retired and let the land to other farmers during the war. The land they owned in Cott Lane has now been developed.

Bay View Farm, originally called 'New Buildings', was farmed by William Parsons and his son Tom. Later the farm was taken over by Tom and May and their daughter Janet. They had land around the farmhouse, at Tixwell and at Baggy. The original barn at Tixwell was home to barn owls who squawked and hooted as we passed on our way home to Wee Cott. Tom's first tractor was a standard Fordson with spade lugs which had to be protected by bands if he wanted to take it on the road. The land around Bay View Farm is now run by George and Janet Hakin and family as a caravan and camping site. They have a daughter Joanne and three sons, Jonathan, Neill, and Craig.

Bridge Farm with Geoff Lang c1960

Bridge Farm was home to Bill Kift, his wife and their daughter Violet. Bill farmed land at Cross known as Needlers and also owned Ora Hill where our television mast is now situated. When he retired, the farmhouse and orchard were sold to Arthur and May Brown. Arthur also owned and farmed Ora Hill fields for several years. Although a builder, he was also a keen vegetable grower and I used to help harvest his potatoes when I lived at Combas Farm.

Myrtle Farm, at the bottom of Jones's Hill next to Croyde Motors, was built in 1600 and was owned and run by two brothers Gilbert and Alf Gammon and their two sisters, Doll and Eva. They ran a mixed farm with Devon cattle. Doll and Eva looked after the house and poultry and sold milk, eggs, vegetables and homemade cream from the door. Alf and his wife, who had no children, lived in the adjoining cottage. Their land was mainly in Croyde Bay, behind Ruda Farm. When they retired I used to store potatoes in their barn. After they died, the house and out-buildings were sold and some are now converted into living accommodation. Doll and Eva were popular characters in Croyde pantomimes.

My father outside Myrtle Farm and Myrtle Cottage 1950

Alf Gammon, children unknown and my father c1935

Lundy House, next to Ruda Caravan Park, was also a farm, farmed by George Fowler, he owned some of the land along Moor Lane and retired when I was young. Lundy House is now a holiday let and the surrounding land was sold.

Tidy , Gilbert Gammon and Tom c1935

Ruda Farm was farmed by Bill Reed. When he retired he built Nail Park (now known as Sole Field) on the Croyde Bay Road, Moor Lane. Ruda was taken over by Harry and Bella Shapland and gradually went from a campsite with a few tents to the caravan and camping park it is today. When Harry and Bella retired it was taken over and run by their son Gordon and his wife Mary, and sons Nigel and Ian. It was developed over the years and a fun pool and other attractions installed. After the death of Gordon it was sold to Mr Paul Yates and family and now belongs to Parkdean Leisure who own other caravan parks around the country.

Ruda Caravan Site with Burrows Mead in foreground c1950

67

Fig Tree Farm

Fig Tree Farm situated in St.Mary`s Road was farmed by Ern Clarke, his wife and daughter May, and was originally owned by the Dennis Estate. Some of the land was at Tixwell, on the opposite side of the road and I can remember them bringing loads of corn sheaves down a steep lane beside Berry Cottage at Cross. They had a drag on one wheel, which acted as a brake and made it easier for the horse. Following them, Mr and Mrs Norman and their daughter Joan took over at Fig Tree Farm. Len Reed, his wife and two daughters then moved in and farmed the land, mainly dairy. The house has since been sold several times, been used as a guesthouse and there is now a barn conversion in the yard.

Mill Farm, next to the Manor House Inn, was farmed by Andrew Fowler, his wife and sons Bob, Harry and Clifford. Clifford was very theatrical and told me that when he was sent to fetch the cows, he would take an umbrella (if it was raining) and his camera! Lionel Hookway and his wife took over Mill Farm, which they bought from the Dennis Estate. They ran a mixed farm, mainly dairy, and Mrs. Hookway took in summer guests. It is now a private residence. When Mr and Mrs Hookway retired, I used some of their sheds for storage.

Kittiwell House was owned by Captain Bigge and the land surrounding it was farmed by Lionel Hookway in conjunction with Mill Farm. The land has now been developed into Millers Brook and the Manor House Inn car park. Over the years, Kittiwell House has changed hands many times and is now run as a guest house, also self catering accommodation.

Harold (Bosun) Bale, Tom McCollum, Ken Ley
Arthur Brown on Ford Ferguson Tractor. 1952

Horse and cart standing in Cott Lane c1920

The Miles family, who lived at Cross, owned and farmed land at Baggy. To get to their ground which was approximately a mile away from Cross they reached it by way of Broadway Lane and Ramson Lane. They grew crops of corn and potatoes for sale, and swedes for winter feed for their small flock of sheep. The corn was cut and taken home by horse and cart where it was made into ricks behind their farmhouse, being threshed in the winter. The house is a traditional Devon longhouse, mainly built of stone and cob with a thatched roof. Bill Miles also worked for Isaac`s, cycling long distances to wherever he was required in Devon, helping to maintain the roads and only returning home at weekends. He also used a horse and butt to transport stones from local quarries.

Mr Marshall, who lived at St. Helen's Priory, also owned some land in Cott Lane and Saunton Down. During the war he sold homemade sweets from his home.

Many of the old characters in the parish had nicknames. A retired farmer who lived at Home House was always known as 'Boxer Tucker'. A jolly old character, who always wore breeches and leggings. His brother, who farmed at Manor Farm, Putsborough, was known as 'Champion'. He had a cob which he used to ride across his land, known as Sharplands, from Putsborough to Forda. When working his dogs, his voice echoed across the valley. Apparently he got the nickname because he had a ram which won first prize – a champion!

Another old character was Bob Norman, known as 'Curlew'. He had long white hair and regularly walked the local footpaths.

George Symons, known as 'Pimple', ran the car park at Downend for many years and also owned Ora Stone Caravan Site which has now been developed.

Frank Bagster, who farmed at Baggy Farm for many years was known as 'Jaffa'. When he retired he liked to sit outside and have a yarn with walkers who took a shortcut across the farm.

Champion Tucker

Frank (Jaffa) Bagster and Maria Lewis 1971

Bob Norman 1986

William (Angel) Parsons,   William (Bill) Lewis (my uncle)   1938

William Parsons, known as 'Angel', farmed at Bay View Farm, now the camping and caravan site. When he retired, he was regularly seen around the village with his walking stick. He liked to go to the Manor House Inn for a pint.

St.Mary's Road, note the piles of cracked stone in front of cottages 1920s

Another old character seen working around Croyde was Dick Miles, who lived at Vale Cottage, Cross. Butt loads of large stones from Spreacombe Quarry were dumped in lay-bys around the village. Using a small hammer with a flexible stick, labourers would break these stones into smaller pieces suitable for making the roads, rolled in by a steam roller. For cracking stones the men were paid by the yard. Dick was regularly covered in red dust from the quarry stones and known as 'Red Dick'.

My grandfather was known as 'Cockerleg'. He lived at Hobbs Cottage and was a gardener at Croyde Bay House for Sir Arthur Watson. He stuttered, but after a few pints, courtesy of the visitors in the pub, he could sing without hesitation.

My father, known as 'Humpy', was well-known for his riding school for many years, and for his donkeys that he took onto the beach.

A regular meeting place for some of these old characters, weather permitting, was the surrounds of the surf shop, formerly the butchers shop, where they sat and chatted, argued and reminisced and generally put the world to rights. This was known as the death slab by the younger generation!

Harriet Lewis   *William Lewis*

1870-1913 age 43   *1874-1942 age 68*

My Grandparents

73

Baggy Farm, 251 acres of farmland and the farmhouse (now known as Baggy Hoe) including the headland of Baggy was given to the National Trust in 1939. The donors were the Misses Connie and Florence Hyde, who lived at Baggy House with their brother Edwin. This red brick house, completed in 1893, was built for the Hyde family as a country residence and was the first dwelling to be seen across the bay when arriving into Croyde from Downend. An early resident member of the family was a Doctor Feeney, an accomplished artist. George Bagster told me that when they were young, he and his brothers would be summoned to the Hyde house and measured for suits to be made by a well-known mens outfitters in Barnstaple.

Baggy House c1920

As a boy, I used to deliver newspapers to the Hydes, although I only remember seeing their cook. The family also owned the three other houses situated near the cliff, which housed two gardeners, Bill and Leonard Ley, and Harry White the chauffeur. When the Ley brothers retired, Bill Foster took over as the only gardener.

In my early days working at Baggy Farm, I would often see Miss Hyde taking a stroll out to the slipway on Baggy Point where Mr Hyde kept his boat. George and Bill Bagster told me they would sometimes be invited to join Mr Hyde for a trip in the boat to check on the lobster pots. In the winter they helped to winch the boat from the rocks to the bank above. The slipway and dry area are still visible and accessible by winding steps passing a seat. On the outer rocks beside deeper water, there was a concreted area which the Hyde family used when diving into a large pool. Beyond the pond and wooded area, between the first gate and slip-

74

Edwin Hyde, his two sisters and staff with Bill Ley back right c1915

Baggy Farm

Gwen Dennis 'who later married Michael Killard-Leavey'
and Bill Lane with Mr. Hyde's boat 'Molly'
early 1920s

Mr Hyde preparing to launch 'Molly'

way, some steps were cut out of the rock. These steps led to Feeney's Cave (so-called by the Bagster family) where Dr Feeney would sit and paint, weather and tide permitting. The pond was originally the home of many mallard ducks, which all mysteriously disappeared during the American occupation!

Upon the death of the last surviving sister, the houses were sold; the chauffeur and gardeners' houses to private owners. The main residence was bought by Frank Purcell and partners and converted into a hotel and it was in their possession from 1970 until 1978. Three successive owners ran the hotel until it was sold again as a property investment. In 1993 planning permission was granted to the present owner, Gavin Davis, to demolish the building and re-build a family holiday home.

Mr Hyde looking at bones of the large whale which was washed up on Croyde Beach in 1915.
Only a small part still remains at Baggy Point today.

After leaving Combas Farm, I returned home to live and used to cycle to work at Baggy Farm. My father had sold Wee Cott to Mr. and Mrs. Cuthbert and he built another bungalow, which he called Milkaway, on land at the top of Mill Lane. This was much nearer the village, and is now called Brambles. (Please refer to chapter IV for information on Combas Farm.)

Combas Farm

*My mother
in the kitchen
at Milkaway
1950*

I was originally employed by Frank Bagster, a grand old character who had many tales to tell with a twinkle in his eye. He was a good boss and would sometimes give me a packet of cigarettes as an extra. I remember one of the tales he often told, visitors to the area would ask him: "How often do people fall off the cliff at Baggy Point?" to which he would reply, "Only once, m'dear", with a chuckle.

In 1942 thousands of American soldiers were sent to North Devon and I was told many tales about their occupation of the land on the west side of the farm. The troops built a road through farmland from Putsborough to Baggy Point, past the farmhouse. This track was made of reinforced metal which was rolled out to form a solid base and 2 foot angled spikes were used to keep it in place. It passed straight through walls and hedges and widened gateways. Stones used for the construction were obtained from the quarry on the approach road to the farm. The troops drilled holes and then used explosives to extract the rubble. In one of the fields there were rows of latrines and a large store for wire, stakes, and chestnut paling for fencing.

Baggy Farm and out buildings   1963

The troops occupied all the land from the farmhouse to Baggy Point and constructed concrete pillboxes reinforced with metal rods at various points around the farm, which were used for target practice. Some of these pillboxes can still be seen from the top footpath to Baggy Point. Shells were fired from the Putsborough end of Baggy. Some of them fell short and on one occasion a corn rick was set alight. On another occasion phosphorous bombs fell amongst a crop of kale. Mr. Bagster was told that it was safe to put sheep in the field to eat the kale but unfortunately this was not the case and several of his sheep died.

American ships, loaded with supplies for the troops, anchored under Baggy Point and Dukws were used to transfer the goods to the mainland. On one occasion, in very bad weather and heavy seas, several landing craft capsized and it was thought that about twenty to thirty servicemen were drowned.

One amusing tale concerning the Americans related how, when they first arrived in Croyde in tanks, they stopped to ask Bill Carder the way to Baggy. He directed them up Middleborough Lane, just past the entrance to the beach, on the right. They drove up and as they advanced, the lane became narrower and the banks became higher, resulting in one tank getting stuck and having to be pulled out by another one. Bill Carder, a local character, soon disappeared to relay the tale in the village, because he should have directed them to follow the road to Baggy Point. Even today, the bank on one side of the lane is still low where it was crushed by a tank.

While the American troops were here, Phyllis Miles opened a room at Vale Cottage, Cross and sold coffee, teas and refreshments. Dora Rodd also sold refreshments from her cottage opposite Mill Farm in Croyde.

The majority of the troops were stationed in Braunton, coming to Baggy for training. It was said that on their return to Braunton, marching two by two, a continuous line of men stretched from Baggy Farm, across Croyde Beach to Downend corner. All of this training was in preparation for D-Day. Many of these servicemen were killed on the Normandy beaches which we visited in 2002 with Maria and Mark our American son-in-law.

After the war, when the land was returned to agriculture, the ministry ploughed the fields with a special caterpillar fitted with a steel cab to protect the driver from unexploded shells. In the 1950s, whilst ploughing on the farm, I would occasionally turn up shells, some of which were phosphorous and would catch fire as soon as they came into contact with air. The Americans had dumps around the farm where they threw small arms shells. When I came across them, I would collect the brass and take it to the scrap merchants.

As so many of the walls and gateways had been demolished during the American occupation and training, Dennis contractors moved in to rebuild walls and re-install gateways. Approximately twenty men with dumpers and bulldozers spent all of one winter rebuilding, using tons of stones from Spreacombe Quarry.

Baggy Farm was a mixed farm. When I started work there, they grew approximately six acres of potatoes, ten acres of mangolds and turnips for cattle feed, eight acres of swedes, six acres of cauliflowers, two acres of savoys, half an acre of sprouts for the Christmas market and one acre of hungry gap kale for early spring picking. The cereal crops consisted of approximately fifty acres of barley and five acres of oats. There used to be an Autumn Show every year in the Pannier Market, Barnstaple, where corn merchants and farmers competed for prizes for the best grain for seed and malting. Baggy was well known for its barley and two types of oats, black and golden varieties, and regularly won prizes at the show.

The stock at Baggy consisted of sixty head of beef cattle of all ages and a large flock of breeding ewes, some of which started lambing at Christmas. Then after a break of one month, the rest would start to lamb in March.

Baggy Farm 1964 dipping sheep
George Bagster and me

Some lambs were sold during the spring and summer months and the later lambs were kept over the winter and fattened on swedes, which we strip-grazed by fencing off the crop and moving the wire and stakes each day. These sheep, known as hogs or two-teeths, were sold at about one year old.

There were ten Devon cows that were hand milked twice a day. The milk was taken into the dairy in the farmhouse, strained, cooled and poured into various sized bottles, which were then sealed with cardboard tops. Bill Bagster had a bicycle with a metal crate at the front that held several bottles and he delivered milk to some of the local residents. Later they stopped selling milk, only keeping enough for their own use, and the calves suckled the cows.

They would also buy four eight-week-old pigs, known as weaners, and fatten them to approximately twelve score, keeping one for their own use and selling the rest. Some of the surplus milk and small potatoes were fed to the pigs. These known as 'pigs tatties', were boiled in a large copper, similar to the one at Combas Farm, then mixed with barley meal. This provided enough feed for two to three days. A few chickens, ducks and turkeys were kept for egg production, and the Christmas market.

Russell Bagster collecting seaweed on Croyde Beach for fertilizer c1930

As well as Frank Bagster, his three sons: George, Billy and Russell, Bill Carder, Peter Symons and I all worked full time at Baggy, and sometimes friends and relatives would help at harvest time. Billy kept a pony for riding and I used to ride it at the local hunt. They also had two carthorses, which Russell used mainly for light work and for pulling a butt or cart filled with farmyard manure. This was loaded manually and then spread on the fields using a fork. Later a mechanical dung spreader was used. At that time there were two sheepdogs and my Jack Russell that lived on the farm.

George was married to Joan and, with their daughter Wendy, they lived at West Winds on the main road to Baggy Point. Two of his sisters, Emma and Joan, were not married and lived at the farmhouse, looking after the house and poultry.

As we became more mechanised, less people were needed. North Devon Farmers would arrive once a year with a fore-loader and two tractors with dung spreaders and clear the yard and sheds. Later we had our own fore-loader and spreader.

Baggy Farm 1968
L-R
  Me
  Joan Bagster
  Frank Bagster
  George Bagster
  with Kim the dog

Caroline Lewis, Bess the sheepdog, Kevin Lewis (Cousin) , Maria Lewis.
Baggy Farm 1976

In the early days all the corn was threshed, which would take three to four days during the winter. Later, approximately fifty percent was threshed and the rest combined by North Devon Farmers. When Baggy had its own combine, I would drive it, and all the corn was harvested this way.

Our first combine was bought from Gordon Hernaman. Another was bought from John Potter at Mortehoe and I drove it home. It was a petrol TVO model with a six foot cut. The next was a seven foot diesel model. Another time I went to fetch a corn drill from Thomas` of Bishops Tawton. I was towing it behind my Dexta tractor with no problem until I reached the George Hotel in Braunton. I encountered a dip in the road, whereby the pin flew out, the towbar reared up and the corn drill careered across the road, mounted the pavement and hit the window-sill of Webbers Estate Agents. Fortunately it was lunchtime and few people were on the streets. A passerby helped me to recover the drill, hitch it up, and I continued on my way. Thinking I had had a lucky escape, I got back to the farm only to be told that a member of Webbers Estate Agents had spotted me, and they claimed a few pounds for the damage. Nowadays it would be an offence to use a pin without a safety clip.

Baggy Farm c1978
Making a rick of staw bales
L-R Arnold Comber, Wendy and Paul Dymond, Joan Bagster,
Mick Comber, Me and George Bagster.

CROSS CROYDE.

The field at Forda shown at top left of photograph overlooking Cross

While I was working at Baggy Farm my brother George and I cleared a south facing field at Forda, known as the Brake, which was covered in thick gorse and bracken. It was approximately four acres and we ploughed it with an old Fordson tractor and single furrow plough. We had a problem with the tractor which died on us because it wasn't getting enough oil due to the steep incline. Our next tractor, a petrol tvo grey Ferguson with a hydraulic, required me to sit on the bonnet going up the Brake, in order to keep the tractor from lifting up. We only ploughed or harrowed on the way down. We cultivated this land for a few years, growing potatoes and strawberries also cauliflowers and cabbages in the meadow below until my brother bought a farm at Combe Martin. The land now belongs to Ken and Sheila Sims of Bracken View.

As well as working at Baggy Farm, my wife and I farmed approximately twenty five acres of grassland on the Croyde side of Saunton Down. We kept cattle and sheep and reached this land by way of Somerthing Lane. Some of this land belonged to the Dennis Estate and some to the Thomas family, who lived in a cottage on Croyde Bridge before it was converted to a shop, now Redwood Surf Shop. We also farmed two acres at Buckland, mainly used for corn. This was part of a field divided into large allotments. We also rented half an acre of allotment on the Putsborough road, opposite Thornberry Cottage. This was part of a two and a half acre field divided into five plots, owned by the Dennis Estate. Bill Symonds, Bob Norman, Reg Symons and Len Reed farmed the rest of the field at that time. We rotated the crops we grew here, as we did in other fields we rented around the village. Altogether we had twenty acres of arable, some of which we owned.

Shirley and me picking up potatoes in the paddock at Solefield 1988

For several years my father rented three and a half acres from Mrs Gesregan, on which he kept sheep and cattle. I took over this field in 1980, ploughed it and had crops of strawberries and vegetables. Half way down this field is a pumphouse next to a well and this water was pumped to Solefield before the mains water came to Croyde. I grass-seeded the field some twenty years ago and the water is still used for horses, which now graze the field. Simon Maddocks runs the riding stables at Roylands, Croyde Bay.

On the way to Braunton Wheels Extravaganza
on my 1962 Ford Dexta restored by Ken Sims of Forda

I worked at Baggy Farm for twenty six years and during that time George Bagster took over the running of the farm and was very helpful to me in lots of ways: lending me tractors and implements, combines and sprayers and heavier gear for my land. I kept my Dexta tractor at the farm and used it for the lighter work such as spraying, drilling and mowing grass, also sowing corn and fertilizer. He also gave me the pick of several of the best of the draft (or older) ewes which they normally sold in September. I kept them at Baggy, and then sold them with their lambs the following spring.

When our daughter Maria was three or four years old, she used to help Emma collect the eggs on the farm. As she grew older, she used to help plant potatoes, cauliflowers and savoys. She and I would be on the planter and George would drive the tractor. At harvest time she would drive the cows in from the field, feed them and let the calves suckle. After the calves were put back in their pen, she would let the cows out and wash down the shippen. She also helped to cut

87

cauliflowers and pick up potatoes behind the spinner. George paid her for her help. Maria, and later Caroline, used to love their time at Baggy as they enjoyed the freedom and the animals. Maria was upset when all the animals were sold and subsequently became a vegetarian.

When George retired and we left the farm in 1980, the National Trust let the land at Baggy to the Lang brothers. When they gave it up a few years later, a farmer from Ilfracombe took over. Joe Bowden a farmer from Braunton was the next tenant and now Andrew Cooper farms the land and lives in the farmhouse, known as Croyde Hoe Farm.

Arrowheads and flints found at Baggy between 1954-80

Over the years, many flint artefacts have been found in fields on the farm, ranging from Mesolithic times through to the Bronze Age. I have some fine examples of flint tools including some arrowheads. The most common flints found on Baggy are from the Mesolithic times (Middle Stone Age). Techniques improved dramatically in the Neolithic time (New Stone Age) with carefully worked spearheads and arrowheads.

In the Bronze Age metal tools were still scarce and flint tools were greatly improved, as shown by the barbed arrowhead at the top right of the photograph. The squared off black flint represents the Modern age when flint was still used as the striker in flint lock rifles.

Our last load to the wholesalers 1990

We continued market gardening, supplying several shops in Croyde and Braunton with fruit and vegetables until I had hip replacements. We then gave up the tenancy of several fields and sold the land we owned.

My wife Shirley and I started gardening – at one time we looked after more than forty gardens – some belonging to local residents and some second homes or summer lets, holding the house keys if required.

Looking from Downend across Croyde Bay toward Baggy c1905

Croyde Bay and Baggy Point.

Chapter VII

COASTGUARDS

L/H Coastguard Station c1907

I joined the Auxiliary Coastguard when I was eighteen years old. There were approximately twenty men in total, divided into four sections, each with a numbered armband and one or two officers in charge. We used to practise on Baggy Point using the mast (which is still there) as the mast of a ship. Alf or Gilbert Gammon used to take two horses out to the coastguards station at Pathfields, hitch up the rocket cart and take it to Baggy Point with all of the equipment. After unloading everything, and having everyone in their correct positions, number one would fire the rocket from a launcher. During a practice, the rocket was attached to a drag line so that it was held back and not lost over the cliff. The line had to fall very close to the mast, allowing for the direction of the wind to take it aboard the imaginary vessel. Number five would shout "line held", which meant the line was on board. More ropes were attached which propelled the breeches buoy from ship to shore. The breeches buoy held one person at a time and could float if necessary. When he was young, Daniel Farson got into difficulties off Baggy Point and had to be rescued by the coastguard. Negley Farson gave a cup to be awarded every year to the best coastguard station in a wide area covering North Devon and North Cornwall and competitions were held, which Croyde won on several occasions. By then, a lorry had replaced the horse and cart to transport the equipment. Due to increased use of the helicopter and inshore lifeboat, the large rocket was replaced by a handheld pistol and the heavier equipment was no longer used.

Auxiliary Coastguards c1956

Eric Perryman,   Harry Fowler,   TomLang
Ken Ley, Harty Tucker, Fred Gammon, Bill Bagster, Jack Boucher, Ern Lang
George Bagster, Bill Symonds, Harry Easton, Charles Lewis, Reg Summers,
                                          Arthur Brown, Fred Treasure.
Tom McCollum, Fred Crow (full Time) Tom Parsons, me, Mickey Howard

We practised cliff rescue using a stretcher and dummy and patrolled our area in the coastguard Land Rover.

We were also involved in wet winching with 22 Squadron at Chivenor, this was an exercise to teach RAF trainees survival techniques in water. The helicopter lowered a man fitted with a strop and attached to a cable down into the sea. When released from the strop, the trainee would inflate a dingy, which he then had to haul himself into, this could be a challenge in rough sea. The helicopter meanwhile, would leave the area and this is where the coastguards took over, positioning ourselves in a lay-by at Saunton Down and monitoring the situation until the helicopter returned and recovered the trainee and equipment. The coastguards were in radio contact with the helicopter crew at all times during this manoeuvre to report any difficulties.

Auxiliary Coastguards 1980
John Symonds, me, Alan Bates preparing for cliff exercise

There were also resident full-time coastguards in Croyde. They lived at Pathfields before transferring to Moor Lane. During rough weather, either a full-time or Auxiliary Coastguard would keep watch from Baggy Point. There was one lookout on the point which was abandoned due to cliff erosion. The last one to be used was situated on the north side of Baggy Point, around the corner from the mast. Watches were discontinued due to the streamlining of the coastguard service and the lookout was demolished.

I received my long service medal after twenty five years and retired from the Auxiliary Coastguard Service in 1988 after thirty three years. I also have the long service medals awarded to my father, my uncle Bill Lewis and my grandfather. The Auxiliary Coastguard now have an office and garage for their vehicle and equipment off Lane Head Close.

One wreck that I can remember was the Monte Gurugu which broke-up in heavy seas north west of Baggy in 1949. Bill Shapland and I went down to Putsborough Beach the next morning and saw all the lifeboats and other debris which had washed ashore. One such boat had washed ashore at Woolacombe Sands, containing one man and two bodies. Ilfracombe lifeboat picked up a boat with eighteen men and Appledore lifeboat picked up three bodies.

Coastguard Long Service medals awarded to the Lewis family

| *William Lewis* | *William Lewis* | *Charles Lewis* | *John Lewis* |
| (grandfather) | (uncle) | (father) | (author) |

A good catch at Putsborough c1928
Ern Adams, Tom Parsons, Bill Symonds, Leonard Rodd

Fishing off Croyde or Putsborough Beaches with a long net was enjoyable and sometimes profitable. We generally fished on a calm summer night, two hours back from high tide. The net was pulled 'out-staff' by three people, one carrying the staff over his shoulder and two others pulling ropes in front. One or two people held the net on the beach or 'in-staff'. The net had floats on one side to keep it above the waves and weights on the other side to keep it on the seabed. Those 'out-staff' walked in a semi-circle and gradually made their way back to the beach, usually having three 'drafts' on Croyde Beach. Catches varied but usually consisted of bass, flat fish, dover sole or plaice. We did not have the luxury of wetsuits in those days, so old clothes were worn, which was fine to start with but not so good on re-entering the water for the second and subsequent 'drafts'.

On one occasion, Bill Bagster walked into a deep pit on Croyde Beach whilst on 'out-staff'. He came up spluttering, still wearing his trilby and declared he would never go fishing again!

When I was young, Mr Whitehead, who lived at Beach Cottage, Croyde Bay, supervised the beach and hired out deckchairs. He also worked as a lifeguard as he was a very good swimmer. He paid me two shillings each evening during the summer to pick up litter on the beach. He had always been keen on wood carving

Mr Whitehead's home Beach Cottage (Centre)
and hut on the beach for the life saving equipment. c1935

Mr Jack Whitehead with three new puppets commissioned by Mr Jan Russell,
for his television production on 29th January 1950 of `Red Riding Hood`

as a hobby and after the war, began a career as a puppeteer, making puppets and giving shows all over the country. He also helped present the famous Muffin the Mule programme on television. A new career opened up when Mr Whitehead, then living on the Isle of Wight made a figurehead for a boat a local yachtsman had built to sail to New Zealand. This started a flood of orders for figureheads that kept Mr Whitehead and his wife busy. Mrs Whitehead, who was an artist, decorated much of her husband's work.

Looking through to the old limekiln where tea was served c1930

Before the war, two ladies served tea and refreshments from the limekiln on Croyde Beach. As mains water was unavailable at that time, George and Bill Bagster were paid to fill containers from a spring near Croyde Bay House and carry them over to the tea rooms each evening during the summer months. In the late 1950s when mains water was connected across Lime Kiln field, adjacent to the beach, the kiln was used again for a while, serving snacks and beverages.

At that time, before surfing became really popular, wooden surfboards were used. In the sand dunes, there were a few chalets owned by local people and during the winter gales, they were nearly covered by the sand, having to be dug out in the spring. Eventually they were all taken down or buried.

Croyde Beach Tea Rooms c1930
Once known as the Sunbonnet Tea Rooms

Chalets in sand dunes and parking on beach c1930

The tents in the foreground ,we believe, belonged to the Childrens Special Service Mission , a religious group who used to stay in Croyde. c1948

Croyde Beach c1950

Looking from Downend across Croyde Beach to Middleborough Hill

Surfing has now become big business and this is reflected in most of the village shops, where surfboards and surfing equipment can be either hired or bought.

The village pubs continue to expand, all serving meals. I can remember when all you could buy to accompany your pint was a packet of crisps or a chocolate bar!

All of the small estates or cul-de-sacs in Croyde have been built during my lifetime. Over the years I have worked in most of the fields either hoeing, harvesting or threshing, before they were sold for development. Orchard Grove was originally a well-established orchard, belonging to the Webb family, and a favourite of ours for scrumping apples as it could be entered from Cott Lane or Cloutmans Lane. This also gave us a speedy exit if needed!

The area around Croyde has well-maintained footpaths which are used by locals and holidaymakers alike. Two of my favourite walks are around Baggy Point and across the downs to Saunton, a walk that I enjoy regularly. Croyde attracts holidaymakers of all ages and the view across the beach when approaching the village from Saunton is surely one of the best.

Croyde Beach c1935

My brother Fred

My brother Fred, had served with the 4th Hussars in Germany and was recognised as being an expert horseman. In civilian life he was employed as a heavy equipment operator. In 1967 he was exercising a local horse for point to point racing. When galloping across Saunton Beach the horse tripped and Fred was thrown, he died almost immediately. He was thirty three and left a widow, Pauline and two children, Karen and Kevin.

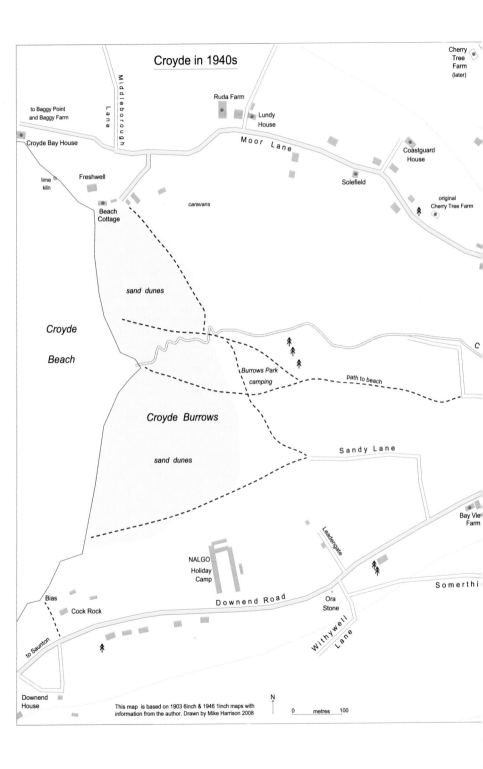

Croyde in 1940s

Cherry Tree Farm (later)

to Baggy Point and Baggy Farm

Croyde Bay House

Middleborough Lane

Ruda Farm

Lundy House

Moor Lane

Coastguard House

lime kiln

Freshwell

Solefield

original Cherry Tree Farm

Beach Cottage

caravans

sand dunes

Croyde

Beach

Burrows Park camping

path to beach

Croyde Burrows

sand dunes

Sandy Lane

Bay View Farm

NALGO Holiday Camp

Leadengate

Bias

Cock Rock

Downend Road

Ora Stone

Somerthi

Withywell Lane

Downend House

N

This map is based on 1903 6inch & 1946 1inch maps with information from the author. Drawn by Mike Harrison 2008

0   metres   100

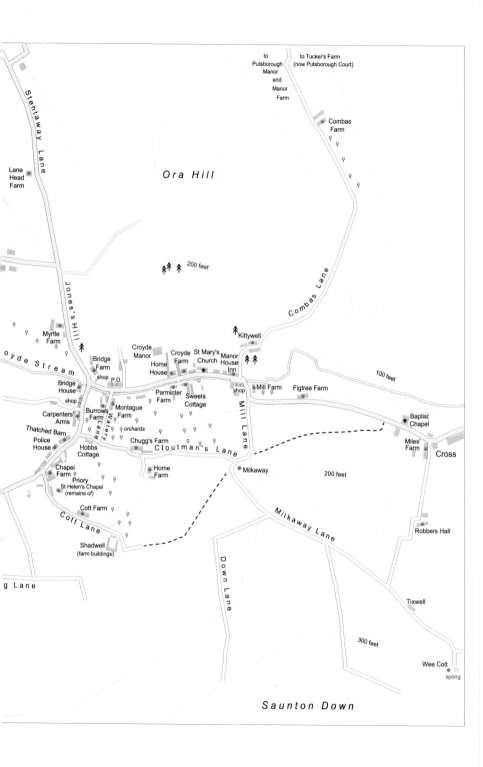